At Issue

Can Busy Teens
Succeed Academically?

Other Books in the At Issue Series:

At Issue

Can Busy Teens Succeed Academically?

Stefan Kiesbye, Book Editor

GREENHAVEN PRESS
A part of Gale, Cengage Learning

Detroit • New York • San Francisco • New Haven, Conn • Waterville, Maine • London

GALE
CENGAGE Learning™

Christine Nasso, *Publisher*
Elizabeth Des Chenes, *Managing Editor*

Articles in Greenhaven Press anthologies are often edited for length to meet page requirements. In addition, original titles of these works are changed to clearly present the main thesis and to explicitly indicate the author's opinion. Every effort is made to ensure that Greenhaven Press accurately reflects the original intent of the authors. Every effort has been made to trace the owners of copyrighted material.

Cover image © Images.com/Corbis

LIBRARY OF CONGRESS CATALOGING-IN-PUBLICATION DATA

Can busy teens succeed academically? / Stefan Kiesbye, book editor.
  p. cm. -- (At issue)
Includes bibliographical references and index.
ISBN-13: 978-0-7377-4286-2 (hardcover)
ISBN-13: 978-0-7377-4285-5 (pbk.)
1. Teenagers--Education (Secondary)--United States--Juvenile literature. 2. High school students--United States--Life skills guides--Juvenile literature. 3. Teenagers--United States--Life skills guides--Juvenile literature. 4. Teenagers--Employment--United States--Juvenile literature. 5. Academic achievement--United States--Juvenile literature. I. Kiesbye, Stefan.
  LB1607.5.C36 2009
  373.0835--dc22
                                                              2008051452

Printed in the United States of America
1 2 3 4 5 6 7 13 12 11 10 09

Contents

Introduction

"Many people simply assume that if you're a top-tier student, then you must be just fine. But a significant percentage of these students who look perfect on paper are dealing with identity issues that can emotionally cripple them," says Alexandra Robbins, author of *The Overachievers: The Secret Lives of Driven Kids*, in an interview with the *Washington Post*. Robbins asserts that stress is entering the lives of younger and younger children who are pressured to succeed in our "overachiever culture." The resulting concern for critics of this phenomenon is that children and teens are unable to grow as individuals and remove themselves from some of the side effects of competition.

In today's society, most would agree that a college degree has become a necessary ticket to a good and well-compensated job, as opposed to a praiseworthy achievement. Often, the degree matters less than the institution that awarded it, and the pressure to achieve admission to a prestigious college or university has become a cultural norm. Get into a good college—a highly ranked public university, or, even better, an Ivy League school—and doors will open for you. Fail to secure admission to Harvard or Princeton, and you qualify for only a second-tier career. These are some of the realities and concerns facing teens today.

The results of such social expectations are stressed teenagers, trying to schedule activities for every available time slot. From volunteerism, to sports, to part-time jobs, teenagers' time is spent like currency to fatten the portfolios college admissions officers will review. Yet often the teenagers' hearts are not in the projects, and stress can lead to eating disorders, depression, and even suicide. Robbins, thinking back on her own school days, says, "Was it overwhelming at times to be a high school student? Sure. But was it at the frenzied level it is now?

Definitely not. That's partly because of the increase in numbers: in only five years the number of students applying to college rose by 1.2 million."

Her sentiment is mirrored by college admissions officers. CBS has reported, "The nation's universities have never been more selective. At top schools like Harvard, Princeton, Northwestern, and Stanford only one in 10 of the highly qualified applicants have a chance at being accepted." Reed College president Colin Diver told CBS, "Over the last five years we've almost doubled the number of applications and we've obviously made it harder to get in here. . . . They're trying every trick in the book, to try to attract the very best students so yes, it's a very competitive environment right now." Considering the enormous struggle for college admission, many contend that the competitive environment is eroding the ideal high school experience: a time to figure out one's interests, a time to make friends and socialize, a time of scholastic nourishment with enough leisure to develop one's own ideas and pursue them.

Yet Jay Matthews, who covers education for the *Washington Post*, disagrees with the assessment that a new overachiever culture has taken hold. He writes:

> According to the National Assessment of Educational Progress, a national achievement test, reading and math scores for 17-year-olds have been stagnant the last 30 years. One of the reasons for this, many educators say, is that students, educators and parents have bought into the notion popularized by Robbins and other social critics that American teenagers have too much schoolwork and should be allowed instead to read for pleasure and watch the sunset and think deep thoughts.

Supportive studies have shown that average American teenagers do only about an hour of homework every night and still make it into college. The remaining time is often spent in front of the television or the computer, for up to 3.5 hours a day.

While Robbins argues that the competitive academic environment is eroding teenagers' emotional and social health, Matthews contends that students' neglect of academic activities is contributing to a lack of scholastic improvement. A compromise may, therefore, call for a balance of students' academic and leisure activities in order to promote intellectual as well as emotional and social success. Robbins reports that "overachiever culture has changed the school environment so that it is a two-tiered system: you're either a high-achieving student, or you're not. There's no middle ground anymore, and 'average' students tend to get overlooked and slip through the cracks."

While the extremes Robbins describes are difficult to attend to, all students need balanced goals and parents' and mentors' help to achieve them to find both academic and personal fulfillment. We should expect students to do well on tests and to strive for college admission, but the pressure and competition should be manageable and encourage students to succeed. Perhaps a balance of priorities can help to find a middle ground, where learning and pleasure share space in the same educational career.

1

Teens in the Workforce

Alison Morantz

Alison Morantz holds a PhD in economics from Harvard University and a JD from Yale Law School.

While working part-time might be detrimental to education, a job also can provide students with the necessary skills for a successful career. Some students even discover careers they would otherwise not have pursued. Teenagers often work to be able to afford cars, clothes or other luxury items, but most earn less than two thousand dollars a year. Job safety, however, is a big issue, as teens are more often injured on the job than adults are. In addition, many employers do not follow teen labor restrictions. Research is inconclusive, but teenagers might benefit from part-time jobs because they can create a vision of life after school and become successful, responsible adults.

Emily Payet, an outgoing high school sophomore, spends about fifteen hours each weekend serving customers from behind the counter of a large deli and bakery in East Boston. Many of her friends from school work there, too. On some Saturdays, she comes in as early as 5:30 A.M. and spends several hours helping to prepare the food. After the store opens, she stands behind the counter selling deli items and baked goods. Hired at $6 an hour, she asked her boss for a raise nine months later and was delighted when he offered her $7.50.

Emily considers herself "lucky to have the job," but says it also has some major downsides. "For one thing, we don't get

Alison Morantz, "Teens in the Workforce," *Regional Review*, Spring 2001. Reproduced by permission of the Federal Reserve Bank of Boston.

any breaks, not even fifteen minutes. Just standing on my feet for eight or sometimes ten hours, there are times when my feet kill [me]. . . . Also, my back hurts now because I do a man's job sometimes, like lifting four gallons of milk in crates and heavy boxes." Nevertheless, she feels she is learning important job skills. "I connect with the public a lot, and sometimes they give you an attitude. As much as you want to give them an attitude back, you can't. Here is what my boss says: 'The customer is always right.'"

Learning Job Skills

Work is a pervasive facet of teenage life. Roughly one-third of 16- and 17-year-olds are employed in any given week during the school year, with about 80 percent holding a job at some point during their junior or senior years. For many teens and their parents, the benefits of working are self-evident. Part-time jobs are one of the surest ways to teach kids important job skills; learning early how to balance school and work may help kids balance competing commitments later on. The time teens spend on the job is generally time they don't spend on criminal activity or dangerous forms of recreation. And, as Emily Payet points out, holding a job gives teens spending money over which they have complete control. "It just gets tiring after a while to ask your parents for money all the time. . . . It's better having your own money. That way you can do what you want with it."

Some teens even discover lifelong careers. "My board of directors is composed of 41 industry leaders," notes Peter Christie, Executive Vice President and C.E.O. of the Massachusetts Restaurant Association. "Many started out in entry-level positions in the fast-food industry. . . . I myself started as a dishwasher in a diner, and then went back twenty years later and bought that diner." Some unusual jobs may even give students entré into careers they would not have considered otherwise. Irene Brand was thinking about a career in journalism before she landed a summer job working with animals at the New England Aquarium. "I never thought about doing this kind of work," said the 16-year-old from Dorchester, Massachusetts. "I might want to continue doing it after I finish school."

On the other hand, working in junior high and high school can carry special risks. Youth and inexperience tend to make teenagers especially vulnerable to workplace injuries and other safety hazards. Coworkers may "educate" teens about alcohol, drugs, and other high-risk activities; extra spending money may encourage them further. And students worn out from too many hours on the job may have trouble keeping up with homework and focusing on classroom instruction. This raises concern that, despite the benefits, teens could even wind up worse off in the long run, with lower-paying jobs and less opportunity than if they had concentrated time and attention on school, athletics, or other after-school activities.

About 60 percent of all working teens work in retail stores and restaurants.

Teen Workers: A Snapshot

As anyone who has bought groceries, ordered fast food, or shopped at a retail store can attest, teens are an important source of labor in many sectors of the U.S. economy. Although well over half of teens report having held some type of job by age 14, the majority performed only "freelance" jobs like babysitting and lawn mowing. Starting at age 15, however, an increasing number of teens take on jobs as regular employees. During any given school week between 1996 and 1998, almost 3 million 15- to 17-year-olds had jobs, while about 4 million teens are employed during the summer months.

The number of hours that teens work also rises with age, although precise estimates vary. According to the National

Longitudinal Study of Adolescent Health, 12 percent of ninth-graders work 15 hours or more per week. This proportion jumps to 42 percent in the eleventh grade. By senior year, a whopping 56 percent of all students are juggling schoolwork with a 15-hour-plus workweek, and almost a quarter are working 30 hours or more. Minority and low-income teens are less likely to be employed than white teens and those from middle- and high-income families. But employed African American and Hispanic teens are likely to work longer hours.

Such part-time employment is not a new phenomenon, particularly for teenage boys. More than a quarter of 16- and 17-year-old males who attended school in 1947 were also members of the labor force, note psychology professors Ellen Greenberger and Laurence Steinberg. Today about 60 percent of all working teens work in retail stores and restaurants. Eating and drinking establishments make up the lion's share of employment, followed by grocery and department stores. Just under one-quarter are employed in the service sector, including entertainment, recreation, domestic labor, and health care. The remainder are distributed among agriculture, manufacturing, construction, and other industries. Minority teens are more likely than whites to hold service sector jobs; teens from low-income families are disproportionately likely to work in agriculture, manufacturing, and construction.

The typical working teen does not earn vast sums. More than half earned under $2,000 per year in 1997–98. Almost one-third earned between $2,000 and $5,000 per year, and only a small group (under 10 percent) earned more than $5,000. Like Emily Payet, the majority cite the desire for spending money as their primary reason for working—not the need to support themselves or supplement family income. In a study conducted by the Massachusetts Department of Public Health, more than three-fourths of teens said "spending money" was the chief motivation. In contrast, 26 percent indicated that they worked "to support themselves," and 19 percent said they contributed part of their earnings to family expenses. (That most working teens come from middle-class homes could partly explain such findings.) As Irene Brand, the teen employed at the New England Aquarium noted, "If I am working for the money, I'll spend it the way I want." Most of teens' earnings appear to go to their own expenses, such as clothing and entertainment, according to a recent study published by the U.S. Department of Labor.

Safety on the Job

If nothing else, child labor laws are designed to protect teens from physical harm by limiting where and when they are allowed to work. For this reason, one might expect that a teen's chance of getting injured on the job would be lower than that of an adult. Surprisingly, however, most studies come to the opposite conclusion. The National Institute for Occupational Safety and Health has calculated that roughly 200,000 adolescents are injured on the job each year, a rate for 15- to 17-year-olds of five injuries per 100 full-time-equivalent workers; by comparison, the rate for workers over 16 was just under three. And the fatality rate among employed 16- to 17-year-olds was only slightly less than that of 20- to 24-year-olds (3.5 compared to 3.9 per 100,000 workers) even though child labor laws seek to ban minors from the most life-threatening jobs.

Working teens' self-reports seem to reinforce these statistics. Between 17 and 50 percent of working teens described having been injured on the job, according to a recent Institute of Medicine report, with between 7 and 16 percent reporting injuries serious enough to require medical attention. As the study's authors concluded, "Typical 'teen jobs' cannot be assumed to be safe. . . . [Various] factors may place younger workers at greater risk than adults confronted with similar hazards."

Some industries appear to be more dangerous than others. A cluster of recent studies has found that manufacturing and construction firms have unusually high rates of nonfatal injuries. Construction is especially dangerous, causing 14 percent of occupational fatalities among youths under 18 years of age, even though it employs less than 3 percent of working adolescents. The states of Washington and Connecticut have identified public-sector jobs (including summer jobs programs) as being especially risky for adolescent workers. And the Massachusetts Department of Public Health also recently declared trucking, warehousing, and retail bakeries to be high-injury industries.

Adolescent boys are injured at higher rates than their female peers, with males accounting for 90 percent of teen deaths on the job.

Agriculture, which gets "special treatment" under federal and most state laws, is far and away the most life-threatening sector. Although just 8 percent of employed adolescents aged 15 to 17 years work on farms, agriculture accounts for 40 percent of all work-related deaths for children under 17.

The hazards seem to be greatest for older teens and for boys. Sixteen- and 17-year-olds have higher rates of injury than younger workers. This may be linked to the fact that teens under 16 are subject to working hours restrictions, and some states go even further than the federal laws to protect young teenagers from hazardous work. But it could also be that older teens have an inflated sense of their own abilities, or that employers give them more hazardous tasks.

Adolescent boys are injured at higher rates than their female peers, with males accounting for 90 percent of teen deaths on the job. Although it is true that boys are more likely to be working in the most hazardous jobs, they also seem to have higher injury rates even within occupations.

Problem Behaviors

According to conventional wisdom, jobs smooth the transition to adulthood by teaching teenagers responsibility, maturity, and professionalism. So one might expect adolescents who work to be generally more disciplined and well behaved than their nonworking peers. Surprisingly, research does not tend to support this conclusion.

A number of studies have found that high school students with jobs—especially boys who work long hours—are more likely to get into various forms of trouble than their nonworking peers. For example, a 1993 study by University of Michigan psychologists Jerald Bachman and John Schulenberg found that boys working more than 30 hours a week were more likely than those working fewer hours (or not at all) to smoke, use drugs or alcohol, and get into trouble with the police, although a later study suggested that this was only true for those already "at risk" for delinquency. Half a dozen other studies published in the 1990s found that working more than 20 hours a week is associated with a greater likelihood of using cigarettes, alcohol, marijuana, and cocaine, regardless of income level, race, and prior substance abuse.

Almost by definition, students who work have less time left to sleep and do homework.

There is no clear consensus on how to interpret these findings. On the one hand, it is possible that employment has a real detrimental effect on teens' behavior. Working may encourage youthful misconduct by increasing levels of day-to-day stress, exposing teens to risky behavior, and giving them an inflated sense of their own maturity. But it is also possible that work itself is not the root cause. It could be that teens who regularly use drugs and alcohol decide to work so that they can better afford their habits, or that teenagers with rebellious inclinations are also attracted to working because it gives them greater independence from parental authority.

Educational Outcomes

Given the importance of education to a teenager's future, the job most important to them may ultimately not be the one that earns them an immediate paycheck, but the one that earns them a high school diploma and the chance to attend college. Do students who work in high school get better or worse grades? Are they more or less likely than otherwise similar students to graduate from high school and enroll in college?

It is easy to see why employment might *lower* students' grades. Almost by definition, students who work have less time left to sleep and do homework. For Emily Payet, juggling her job at the deli-bakery with her schoolwork has been an ongoing struggle. "Basically I have no free time and I never really get to sleep. I'm always tired in the morning—all of the time." Amy Kinney, a high school math teacher in an affluent Boston suburb, said that she and her colleagues often agonize over how to deal with students who show up at school exhausted and unprepared after working long hours. "It is a source of frustration for teachers. . . knowing that school comes second to a lot of kids. . . . [Do you] wake up the kid who you know didn't get home until midnight, and then tried to do his homework [and] is functioning on 4 or 5 hours of sleep?"

Yet there are reasons to doubt whether time spent at work really displaces homework or sleep for the typical student. Although it is hard to get accurate estimates, available studies find that many teens spend less than 10 hours per week on homework—so it is hardly inevitable that work time will crowd out study time. Other studies have found that neither teens' employment status nor the number of hours they work is associated with the number of hours they spend on homework. Perhaps this is because teachers adjust homework assignments to accommodate students' work schedules, or because students themselves consider their work commitments when choosing their courses. Or it might be because students who are less interested and successful in school choose to work.

Gaining early work experience may give students a leg up in the job market once they reach adulthood.

The impact on grades is also hard to pin down. Some studies have found negative effects of employment (or working hours) on grades; others find no significant effect. Interestingly, the impact of working may depend partly on the particular circumstances of the employment experience. For example, employment is positively correlated with grades for teens who report saving their earnings for college. It also appears that making the skills taught in the classroom directly applicable to the workplace can enhance academic achievement, although the evidence is somewhat conflicting. Kinney's experience in the classroom seems to mirror the equivocal nature of such research findings. "I've seen it go both ways," she said. "I've seen a kid who was really not motivated in school get a job and [then] see the importance of school [and] their grades improve. But I've also seen kids who were doing fine in school and then got a job, and their grades fell off the end of the earth. I think the second case is more common. But I think they both happen."

The impact of teen employment on the likelihood of graduating from high school or college seems to be more consistent. The key factor seems to be the number of hours worked. Working long hours is associated with lower educational attainment, although which way the causation runs is hard to say. By contrast, low-intensity work (generally defined as less than 20 hours per week) over a sustained period is associated with an increase in educational attainment, especially among boys. Observes Kinney, "Working maybe 20 hours a week is O.K., but anything over 20, I think is too much. . . . They are sleeping in class, and they fall behind academically because their time is swallowed up at work and they can't study and do homework."

Long-Term Career Success

Gaining early work experience may give students a leg up in the job market once they reach adulthood. Working teens may figure out earlier than their nonworking peers which career would best match their interests and abilities. And they may make professional contacts they can draw on later in life. The experience that teens acquire on the job—such as the ability to convey a sense of professionalism through dress and speech—may make them more attractive to future employers.

But even without such direct benefits, holding a job may enhance long-term economic success. Notes Elaine Augot, who spent eleven years teaching English as a Second Language to high school students in Massachusetts, "Having a job can be positive if it gives kids a vision of what life is going to be like afterward. If you don't like what you are doing because you are working in a boring job, then you may decide that education is the way to go."

A substantial body of research conducted over the last twenty years tends to corroborate this insight. Paid work during high school is generally associated with a greater chance of finding a job after graduation, longer spells of employment, and higher income. Most studies have focused on the first year or two after high school graduation, although a few have documented positive impacts on wages and occupational status that persist up to a decade after graduation.

But a more recent study casts some doubt on the conventional interpretation of these findings. UCLA Professor of Economics V. Joseph Hotz and coauthors tried to control for the possibility that a teen's decision about whether to work while in school is *itself* affected by other unobserved characteristics, such as academic ability or family background, that will also influence their wages later in life. After controlling for such factors, they found that the positive effects of high school employment on adult wages diminished markedly and were no longer statistically significant. In short, there is plenty of evidence to suggest that kids who work in high school are more successful in their adult careers. But it may be premature to conclude that the beneficial effect of the work itself is the driving mechanism. . . .

Regulating Teen Labor

Just a century ago, the United States had no federal law in place that restricted or controlled child labor. Although some states took the lead and passed their own laws as early as the nineteenth century, it was not until 1938 that Congress passed the Fair Labor Standards Act (FLSA), which restricted the ages, hours, and working conditions of school-age workers. The standards embodied in the FLSA are still with us today, but its provisions have evolved over the past sixty years.

An important characteristic of the FSLA is its limited coverage. The Act applies only to workplaces that are engaged in interstate commerce and have annual gross revenue of at least $500,000. Child actors, migrant farm workers, newspaper deliverers, and home wreath makers are entirely exempt. Children working for their parents are also exempt as long as they are not working in occupations deemed especially hazardous, such as manufacturing and mining. The agricultural sector is subject to especially lenient regulation. At age 14, child farm workers can choose their own hours, as long as they don't work while school is in session. Children even younger than 14 can perform hazardous tasks on a farm for their parents, and when they turn 16 years old, they can perform hazardous farm jobs for any employer.

For teens who don't fall under these exceptions, the FLSA regulates two aspects of employment: working hours and hazardous occupations. On school days, working teens 15 years old and under can work up to three hours a day and 18 hours a week. On non-school days, teens 15 years and under can work up to eight hours a day and 40 hours a week. Teens over 15 are not subject to any federal hours restrictions.

Restrictions on hazardous occupations apply to all teens under 18 years in nonagricultural occupations. The current list of banned jobs includes mining, working with explosives, driving vehicles with passengers, roofing, wrecking and demolition, meat packing, and slaughtering. Some argue that the list is incomplete and outdated, omitting occupations such as those that involve exposure to carcinogens and biohazards.

Many Employers Violate Laws

Federal regulations set minimum standards but these can also be overlaid by state laws. Some states have tightened hours restrictions, expanded the list of hazardous occupations, and plugged the gaps in FLSA coverage. Others have chosen standards that are more lax than the federal ones (which means that employers under FLSA are bound by federal law). This two-tiered regulatory structure has created wide disparities in the legal regulation of working teens. So have differences in enforcement. Some states allocate considerable funds; others do not. Some hire enforcement officials who specialize in child labor laws; others leave the task to the officials who enforce every other state labor law.

Some employers have responded to child labor laws by revising their business and personnel practices.

Evidence suggests that violations are common. In 1998, Douglas Kruse and Douglas Mahony estimated that during an average week about 148,000 minors were working in violation of the law. They also found that youths in banned occupations were paid $1.38 less per hour than adults in the same job, saving employers about $155 million per year.

Emily Payet's employer appears to be violating several federal and Massachusetts laws: All workers (not just teens) who work more than six hours in a day are entitled to a thirty-minute meal break, and no worker under 18 years of age is allowed to start work until 6:00 A.M. or to work more than nine hours per day. Whether her employer is deliberately flouting the law is not clear. What is clear is that teens like Emily and her coworkers are often too worried about the reaction of their boss to even raise the issue.

How One Employer Complies

Some employers have responded to child labor laws by revising their business and personnel practices. Market Basket, a supermarket chain based in Massachusetts and New Hampshire, has taken several such measures, according to Jay Rainville, supervisor of store operations. Because a typical delicatessen contains so much age-restricted machinery (such as meat slicers and mechanical trash compactors), the company has decided not to allow employees under 18 to work in the deli. "Our in-house computer keeps track according to the employee's date of birth," Rainville explained, "so if a manager tries to punch someone in to work in the deli who is under 18, the computer automatically kicks them out."

To ensure that teenagers do not work more than the legally permissible number of hours, Market Basket does not schedule its 14- and 15-year-old employees for more than 14 hours a week. "Our policy is more restrictive than the labor laws themselves," said Rainville. "That way, if someone happens to go over their schedule here or there, we are still within the state guidelines. It's kind of a cushion."

2

Working Can Jeopardize Teens' Success in School and Life

Steven Greenhouse

Steven Greenhouse has covered workplace issues for The New York Times *since 1995 and is one of the few remaining full-time labor reporters in the country.*

Many high school students work long hours every week and hurt their academic performance. While many contend that an after-school job teaches teenagers responsibility, several states have sought to regulate teenage work out of fear that American students are falling behind their international peers. Jobs have also eroded teenagers' social and cultural lives and deprived them of the time needed to do homework or participate in extracurricular activities. American teens work more than most other students around the world, and are often too tired from work to go to school or participate in class. By emphasizing lifestyle and consumerism too early, teenagers often hurt their chances for successful careers.

Some weekdays, Alicia Gunther, 17, works past midnight as a waitress at a New Jersey mall, and she readily admits that her work often hurts her grades and causes her to sleep through first period.

Jason Ferry, a high school junior, loves working 30 hours a week as a cashier at a Connecticut supermarket, but he ac-

Steven Greenhouse, "Problems Seen for Teenagers Who Hold Jobs," *New York Times*, January 29, 2001. Reproduced by permission.

knowledges that when he gets home from work at 9:30 P.M. he usually does not have enough time to study for big tests.

For decades, the conventional wisdom has been that it is great for teenagers like these to hold after-school jobs because they teach responsibility, provide pocket money and keep the teenagers out of trouble.

But in a nation where more than five million teenagers under 18 work, a growing body of research is challenging the conventional wisdom and concluding that working long hours often undermines teenagers' education and overall development.

In the most important study, two arms of the National Academy of Sciences—the National Research Council and the Institute of Medicine—found that when teenagers work more than 20 hours a week, the work often leads to lower grades, higher alcohol use and too little time with their parents and families.

Tightening Laws

Influenced by such studies, lawmakers in Connecticut, Massachusetts, Alabama and other states have pushed in recent years to tighten laws regulating how many hours teenagers can work and how late they can work. In Massachusetts, several lawmakers are seeking to limit the maximum amount of time 16-year-olds and 17-year-olds can work during school weeks to 30 hours, down from the current maximum of 48 hours.

In 1998, Connecticut lawmakers reduced the maximum number of hours 16-year-olds and 17-year-olds can work during school weeks to 32 hours, down from 48, and [in 2000] they debated imposing fines on employers who violate those limits. In New York, students that age are allowed to work up to 28 hours during school weeks, while in New Jersey the maximum is 40 hours.

The impetus to tighten restrictions grows largely out of concerns about education, especially fears that American students are falling short on tougher standards and are lagging behind foreign students in comparative tests. While there are myriad reasons for poor school performance, legislators seeking tougher restrictions say American students would certainly do better if they placed more emphasis on work inside school and less emphasis on working outside school.

"We have 16- and 17-year-olds working 40 hours a week on top of 30 hours in the classroom," said Peter J. Larkin, the Massachusetts state representative sponsoring the bill to reduce the number of hours teenagers can work. "Something has to give, and academics seems to be taking a back seat. Sure there is pressure against the bill from employers who need teenage workers to help in a full-employment economy, but many other employers are complaining that the graduates of our high schools are not up to par."

Several studies also found that 16-year-olds and 17-year-olds who work long hours tend to use alcohol more than others in their age group.

With the national jobless rate at 4 percent, near its lowest point in three decades, many employers are eager to hire teenagers and say it would be bad for the economy and for their businesses to limit the number of hours teenagers can work.

In many states, those pushing for tougher restrictions include pediatricians' groups, P.T.A.'s, women's clubs, teachers' unions and the National Consumer League. Those opposing tighter restrictions usually include business groups and the many parents who see benefits in teenagers' working, and who have warm memories of their own first jobs as soda jerks or supermarket clerks.

Negative Effects on Academics

Studies by the National Research Council and professors at Stanford University, Temple University and the University of

Minnesota found negative effects when 16- and 17-year-olds work more than 20 hours a week. These studies concluded that students who work long hours often do not have enough time or energy for homework and miss out on social and intellectual development gained from participating in school clubs and athletic teams.

Several studies also found that 16-year-olds and 17-year-olds who work long hours tend to use alcohol more than others in their age group, largely because they have extra pocket money and copy older co-workers.

"It's probably safe for kids to work 10 hours or less each week when they're in school, but probably not such a good idea for them to work more than 20 hours," said Laurence Steinberg, a professor of psychology at Temple University. "That's when we and other researchers find decreased academic performance and decreased engagement in school."

But many child development experts, teachers and parents said working a modest amount could be valuable for teenagers, teaching responsibility and how to work with others, as well as contributing money to financially strapped households.

"It's a positive thing," said Ted Simonelli, a guidance counselor at Linden High School in New Jersey. "They're learning to be on time, they're learning to be good employees, they're learning a skill that they can trade on when they graduate. Many of the students in the top half of our class work after school."

Work Fosters Discipline

For teenagers in poor city neighborhoods, several studies have found, a job can be especially beneficial because it fosters discipline and provides needed role models.

Supporters of teenage work point to success stories like Josh Hershey, 16, of West Hartford, Conn., who took a job at an after-school child care center because it would help prepare him for the career to which he aspires: teaching. His job helped his schoolwork, he said, because it forced him to procrastinate less and focus more when doing homework.

A new study by the International Labor Organization showed that American teenagers work far more than teenagers in most other countries.

"There are a lot of benefits to students' working in moderation," said Jeylan T. Mortimer, a sociology professor at the University of Minnesota in Minneapolis. "But most sociologists and psychologists would say that it's an excessive load for full-time students to work 25 or 30 hours a week if you think it's important for young people to participate in extracurricular activities, develop friendships and spend time with their families."

A newly released study by the Department of Labor shows that 58 percent of American 16-year-olds hold jobs sometime during the school year, not including informal work like babysitting, while another study shows that one-third of high-school juniors work 20 or more hours each week. The Department of Labor also found that slightly more than two-fifths of 15-year-olds work, as do one in five 14-year-olds.

Several economists said the percentage of teenagers who work has remained at the same level in recent years. Although the statistics are sketchy, these experts said they believed that the number of hours students work has increased, partly because of the tight labor market.

A new study by the International Labor Organization showed that American teenagers work far more than teenagers in most other countries. The study found that 53 percent of American teenagers, from the ages of 16 to 19, work in any given week. In Japan, 18 percent of teenagers aged 15 through 19 work, while in Germany, 30.8 percent of teenagers in that age bracket work.

Too Tired for School

One recent Friday, Alicia, the waitress, a senior at Governor Livingston Regional High School in Berkeley Heights, N.J., acknowledged that she had put in a grueling week. Alicia, who works at Johnny Rockets, a 1950's-style diner at the Short Hills Mall, had missed one day of school that week and arrived late the four other days.

The reason was that she had to work past midnight on Tuesday and Thursday, and that came after working from 10:30 A.M. until 12:30 A.M. on Saturday and Sunday.

"It's fun, and I get a lot of money—I made $240 on Saturday alone," she said, noting that she sometimes earns $40 in tips in an hour when it is busy.

"I'm not doing good in school this semester," Alicia acknowledged, her tone half rueful, half isn't-this-cool. "Because of work, I come into school late or I stay home because I'm so tired."

Joan Tonto, one of Alicia's teachers, said, "She's tired when she comes into school, and by sixth period she's too tired to work on problems in class. I've talked to Alicia about how her job is affecting her in school, and she says, 'I'm making a lot of money, Mrs. Tonto.'"

Teenage labor dates from colonial times, when many youths served as apprentices or helped sow and harvest. But with the nation's rapid industrialization came heightened concerns about teenage labor because of the increased emphasis on education and the many exposés about businesses exploiting children.

Still, many parents urge their children to work, saying it is better than sitting around watching television.

Laura Stifel, whose son Jason Ferry has the 30-hour-a-week supermarket job in Southington, Conn., saw a benefit to teenagers' working. "I think it's great that kids work because it leaves them with less time to get in trouble or be out on the street," she said.

But when she began to worry that Jason's $7.75-an-hour job was taking a toll on his grades, Ms. Stifel barred him from using his car until he got his grades back up.

In the summer of 1999, a 16-year-old Southington High School student working at an amusement park died when he stepped too close to the amusement ride he was tending and was dragged underneath. About 70 teenagers die each year in work-related accidents, and safety experts say these accidents occur because teenage workers often receive little training or supervision.

Federal regulations bar 12-year-olds and 13-year-olds from working in most jobs, with one exception being delivering newspapers. Federal rules prohibit 14- and 15-year-olds from working more than three hours or past 7 P.M. on school days. The federal government places no restrictions on the hours 16- and 17-year-olds can work, leaving the matter to the states.

Several studies have found that 20 percent to 30 percent of teenage workers contribute to family expenses.

Likes Hiring Teens

Jeffrey Ellenberg, who owns a dry-cleaning shop in West Hartford, likes hiring teenagers.

"We used to have quite a few more high school students working," he said. "Unfortunately, in this economy we can't get more of them. The advantage is you can train them to do what full-timers do, but you don't have to pay them the full-time wages and benefits."

At Mr. Ellenberg's shop, Rebecca Gohsler, 16, works two or three afternoons a week behind the counter and 10 hours on Saturdays. Although Rebecca's guidance counselor frets that Rebecca's job is pulling down her grades and pulling her away from extracurricular activities, Rebecca sees her $8-an-hour job as one of the best things in her life. She likes the spending money, likes chatting with customers and likes the sense of independence.

Rebecca, who hopes to become a marine biologist, said her job sometimes undercuts her schoolwork. "If I just came home from work and I have a paper to write, there is a chance I might not spend as much time on it or put in enough effort," she said.

Many educators say parents should crack down on their teenagers' jobs if grades start to languish. Carol Hawkins did just that last spring, ordering her son Jon, 16, a junior at Governor Livingston High, to cut back his 20 hours a week pumping gas when his grades started to suffer.

"This year I've been able to manage my work and my school better," Jon said. "But sometimes I still have to study until 2 in the morning."

Several studies have found that 20 percent to 30 percent of teenage workers contribute to family expenses. Most use their earnings for cars, gasoline, clothes, cosmetics, cell phones, pagers and movies.

Dawne Naples, a guidance counselor at Southington High, said she advised Jason Ferry, when his grades were suffering, that it was unwise to work 30 hours a week, largely to pay for his car and gasoline. "'The car will get you around town,' I told him, 'but what's going to get you beyond Southington High?'" she said.

3

Parents and Schools Can Guide Teens' Employment Decisions

Joan Kuersten

Joan Kuersten is a frequent contributor to Parent Teacher Association.

While working part-time might be beneficial, it is easy for teenagers to work too many hours and neglect friendships or exploring intellectual interests. Parents should investigate the jobs their teens are applying for and step in as soon as their children display negative reactions to working after school. Schools can also help students tie in their work experiences with their education. It is up to parents and schools to guide teens toward a satisfying future.

Parents may wonder at what price their sons and daughters are working part-time jobs.

Are their teenagers reaching their academic potential? Are they striking a healthy balance between homework, a part-time job, and social life, including the pursuit of interests? Do they need to work to help with household expenses? Or are they working to buy nonessentials such as cars, designer clothing, CDs, and concert tickets to keep up with their peers?

Although some experts in human development say paid work can be beneficial to teens—introducing them to the adult world and sometimes reinforcing what they learn in

Joan Kuersten, "Teens and Part-Time Jobs: At What Price?" *Parent Teacher Association*, February 2008. Reproduced by permission of National PTA.

school—problems arise when young people work too many hours. Kusum Singh, an education professor at Virginia Tech in Blacksburg, Virginia, conducted two separate studies on the effect of part-time work on high school students' academic achievement. She found that students who worked 15 or more hours a week while in school showed a decline in grades and performed less well on standardized tests. These students also were less likely to take more demanding courses, particularly higher level math and science courses. According to the U.S. Department of Labor, high school students ages 15 to 17 work an average of about 17 hours a week during school months, an amount that could jeopardize their school performance.

Not only can long workweeks have a negative impact on academic performance, but also they can take away from the opportunity to build friendships and explore interests that could enhance a teen's intellectual and emotional development. Teens have to realize their primary job is getting a good education, and it's the parents' job to see that their teens understand that, says Bryan Shore Fraser, associate director of the National Institute for Work and Learning in Washington, D.C.

Advice for Parents

Parents have the responsibility to establish the number of hours their teenager can work, allowing those hours to increase if he or she maintains good grades, according to Robert Billingham, associate professor of human development and family studies at Indiana University. Fraser agrees, recommending that parents limit their teen's work hours during the school months to 10 hours a week, with the majority of those hours disbursed over the weekend.

Fraser also advises parents to learn as much as possible about their son's or daughter's prospective job, including the type of work he or she will perform, employer expectations, and the pay. Although money may be one of the principal motivators for wanting a job, she says parents should emphasize to their child that he or she shouldn't take a job just for the money, especially if it's the first job to come along.

In addition, parents should help their teens manage the money they make on the job. Fraser recommends that parents suggest their son or daughter put a portion of each paycheck into a savings account, perhaps for college or for a desired item that requires a bigger expenditure of funds.

Once their teen has begun working, parents ought to remain alert to signs that the job may be having a negative impact. Such signs include diminishing interest in school or extracurricular activities, which formerly were sources of self-esteem and enjoyment, and spending less and less time with friends and family members. If signs such as these present themselves, parents need to step in.

What Schools Can Do

Fraser commented that schools and school professionals could do a lot to make jobs meaningful and educational for students, such as working with local businesses to provide students with jobs that have greater career potential. "Potential employers can be invited to mentor high school students and even to help develop a school-to-work curriculum," she said.

Teachers, too, can connect their students' work experiences to school, and vice-versa. For example, a math teacher might suggest students bring to class problems from their part-time jobs that require mathematical reasoning to see how the students solve them.

Why Teens Work

A job may not always be a rite of passage to adult responsibilities. In the first half of the 20th century, most working teens contributed to household expenses and/or saved their money, according to *Selling Out America's Children: How America Puts Profits Before Values—and What Parents Can Do.*

Not so these days. The book's author, David Walsh, writes that most of today's teenagers do not contribute to the family. Instead, they spend their money on entertainment and other personal items. Those who do save their money often do so to purchase a car.

Despite the fact that many teens work to provide themselves with disposable income, which many people frown upon, the reality is that a growing number of high school students are going to hold part-time jobs. It's up to parents and schools to make the work experience more manageable, educationally valuable, and ultimately more satisfying.

4

Teens with Jobs Are Highly Stressed

Julie Grant

Julie Grant is a journalist specializing in science and the environment.

In order to get into the college of their choice, many teens work hard to build the kind of résumé admissions officers are looking for. That means putting in hours volunteering, participating in sports, and working part-time. More teenagers work today than ever before, and they are in danger of turning into mini-adults, with schedules busier than those of their parents. Without parental oversight, teens are in danger of overextending themselves and succumbing to career pressures at an early age.

Teenagers today are busy. They often have more homework and feel more pressure than past generations to participate in extra-curricular activities. In addition, many high-schoolers today hold jobs after school to make money.

Some students at Akron's Firestone High School [in Ohio] are so busy, they eat lunch at their desks during class. Guidance counselor Debbie Christy says many teens keep their plates so full because they're competing for acceptance and financial aid to top colleges. They are, in effect, building resumes:

CHRISTY: "It's no longer just the grades and their standardized test scores. It's involvement in the community, it's

Julie Grant, "Working Teens," *WKSU News: Teenagers: The Millennial Generation,* December 15, 2004. Reproduced by permission.

leadership, it's involvement in extra clubs and activities. It's a whole set of commitments that they're looking for in a well-rounded student and it's very competitive. And a lot of our student body is interested in the selective schools."

Nationally, more than a third of 16- to 19-year-olds work.

Mark Wisberger is another guidance counselor at Firestone. He tells students not to even bother including a job on their college applications. But it doesn't stop them from working:

WISBERGER: "And with all the different criteria that Debbie was talking about to get into schools, I would put working a part time job at the very bottom of that list. I think over the past ten years, I've seen an increase in the number of students who work part-time, for sure. And it does take a big bite out of being a high school student and the whole high school experience. We've talked a lot about how they have jobs to support their cars and cars to support their jobs. They do spend, in my opinion, way too much time worried about part-time jobs after school."

Wisberger says teen workers often seem more like mini-adults because they worry about jobs and paying bills rather than homework and school activities. Nationally, more than a third of 16- to 19-year-olds work.

Briana is a friendly 17-year-old. She's standing behind the customer assistance desk at a chain drug store, where she works 30 hours a week:

BRIANA: "I've worked here a little over a year."

And she's had to give up some things:

BRIANA: ". . . I wanted to play volleyball, but work and sports are really hard to do with my hours."

JULIE GRANT: "Why do you work?"

BRIANA: "Why do I work? To have money so I can buy stuff. So I can buy a car and insurance and everything, extra stuff for myself."

Jobs Reduce Time for School

Briana gives a double thumbs up when asked if she's saved enough money for the car she wants. But she's put in some long days for it. School started at seven this morning . . . and she'll finish her work here at ten tonight. Then she'll do her homework.

GRANT: "Do you feel like homework is secondary to everything else?"

BRIANA: "Um, kind of. But I'm getting straight A's, so it's good, I'm trying to keep up my grades. I really push myself to do good."

Firestone High School English teacher Judy Harrison says many of her students work:

HARRISON: ". . . and not just my seniors. I have a lot of sophomores that have jobs and they come in and they're tired because they work 20-hours a week or more. And their schoolwork suffers. I don't care what anybody says."

Some wider research shows potential positive and negative effects of teens working. 15 hours per week seems to be a threshold. Beyond that, students often have lower grades, higher dropout rates, and are less likely to go to college. Jeremy Staff is a sociology professor at Penn State University who has studied teenagers and work. He says there are different views about how jobs affect students:

STAFF: "Critics of teenage work argue that youth who work at a younger age may adopt more adult-like leisure activities and spending patterns from these particular jobs which can lead to things like early dating, alcohol and drug use, and even possible school misconduct or problems within school."

Abuse on the Job

Guidance counselors say many teens have had a hard time saying no to their employers when asked to work long hours. Jeremy Staff's research partner, Christopher Uggen of the University of Minnesota, is surprised by the number of undergraduates who say things about being mistreated while working in high school:

UGGEN: "'Boy, I was really victimized on that job.' Or 'There was this creepy guy at the ice cream store who would corner me and do all these things to me and I didn't do anything about it.'"

But some studies show that work can help young people, with things such as time management. Staff says students seem to benefit from jobs with structured adult supervision and a clear connection to academics.

Andrea is a 17-year-old high school junior who works at McDonald's up to 30 hours a week. She says it helps her in ways beyond money:

ANDREA: "Yes, it really does. It helps me manage my time and to prioritize, what's more important school or work?"

GRANT: "What's more important, school or work?"

ANDREA: "School. Because I gotta go to school so I won't be working at McDonalds the rest of my life."

Teenagers . . . are turning out to be a highly stressed group.

Andrea plans to go to college. But she lives with her older sister and all her work money goes toward the rent and other bills. Like many teenagers, she believes she needs to join some extracurricular activities to earn a scholarship:

ANDREA: "I wanted to do drill team. They haven't had tryouts yet, but I'm thinkin' about trying out when they do have tryouts for drill team. But then that's gonna cut off from my work. You know. Then there's the prioritizing part. Do I wanna work for McDonalds that's not gonna help me pay for college or do I want to go to school and do extracurricular activities so that I can go to college?"

Jobs Hard to Come By

But Andrea may be lucky to even have a job. Andy Sum, director of labor market studies at Northeastern University, says the job market for teens is tough right now:

SUM: "We've never seen . . . To be honest with you, we've never seen such a low rate of employment. Whether year-round or during the summer. This is the lowest employment rate for teenagers since we've been collecting this data, which goes back to 1948. It's never been this bad."

Teenagers, especially in the inner city, now have to compete with older workers, illegal immigrants, and college students for low wage jobs. Professor Sum says the federal government used to subsidize hundreds of thousands of jobs for inner city teenagers. But that's dried up in recent years. He's concerned about the long-term effects, especially for those who drop out of high school expecting to get a job:

SUM: "The more work you do when you're a teenager, the more you'll work when you're 20–24. The more I work when I'm a teenager, the better my wage is going to be when I'm 20–24. But if you want to know the kids who are worst off, it's the kids not in school, not working when they're 17, 18, 19. That is the best predictor of you being poor and dependent when you're 25–29 years old. So kids who don't get any kind of start on the labor market leave school, don't go college; those kids I guarantee to be your underclass of the future."

While they're teenagers, Millennials are turning out to be a highly stressed group . . . those who cannot find jobs or those who can.

5

Extracurricular Activities Allow Teens to Gain Social Skills

Jennie Kelley

Jennie Kelley is a contributor to Helium, an online community that shares information on a wide variety of topics.

Extracurricular activities teach busy teens necessary social skills and how to manage their time appropriately. Involved students have a better chance of receiving college scholarships and will have acquired the discipline needed to succeed. Yet students should also enjoy their activities and be open to fields of work and volunteerism unrelated to school.

Participation in extra-curricular activities will foster creative, social and physical skills that are desirable qualities to colleges and future employers. Involvement can strengthen self-esteem, build lasting friendships and create a lifetime of memories. These activities help define you in a different way than academic study will. Academics requires so much of a teen's attention that subjects become jobs. Even a student who loves to read in [his or her] spare time may find that assigned reading for an English class is work. Extra-curricular activities can provide a much-needed break from the academic grind.

Surprisingly, there is sufficient argument that students who are involved in extra-curricular activities earn better grades than students who are not. Parents may argue otherwise, and with good reasons. If a student's evenings are spent playing a sport or rehearsing a play, when will he or she have time to complete homework and study for tests?

Time Management Is Key

However, students who have active lives learn very quickly how to manage their time. Procrastination is not an option for a student whose days are busy and structured. Students are much more likely to study during specified hours of down time than another student who "has the entire weekend, so right now I'll just play with my Wii."

Better grades can ... stem from the discipline that extracurricular activities teach.

Along those lines, students learn organizational skills from having to wisely budget their time. Calendars are necessary tools, not only for busy teens, but for busy adults, too! Learning how to use one properly is a fantastic skill to master, both in the classroom and after graduating. Parents can aid their teen in creating and maintaining the family calendar by allowing them to write practice schedules, due dates and study group meetings. It's fun, it keeps family members in the loop, and effectively maintains household sanity.

Better grades can also stem from the discipline that extracurricular activities teach. Good coaches do not respond well to poor excuses for missing practices. Failing in a school subject generally hurts only the student. Failing at a group activity affects everyone. Involved students learn this truth quickly, and loyalty to themselves and teammates becomes an important priority.

Teamwork is another part of discipline and a very necessary skill. Understanding how to work well with others can guarantee a lifetime of positive relationships. In extracurriculars, students learn to encourage others, lift others' spirits, celebrate wins and learn from losses. Teamwork creates a humble nature, when we know that a success is not solely ours to take credit for, just as losses are not only our responsibility. We learn that camaraderie is as important in high school as it will be in college, at a job, and within our own families. Teamwork is well applied to studies. Group activities will be well monitored by the active students who already know how to share, delegate and carry their own weight!

If no school activities look interesting, try volunteering.

Improved Grades

I work for a theatre company that participates in a theatre program for urban high school students who are considered "at risk." The school we chose was a school designated for [assistance], who administrators referred to as, "the worst of the worst." They were students expelled from the local public school and had nowhere else to go. However, each student involved in our program showed a marked improvement in grades. Even their attitudes towards school softened. Theatre provided these students an outlet—a chance to pretend to be someone else for a little while. And, at the end, eight students who could barely construct a complete sentence performed Shakespeare's *Hamlet* for their families, peers and teachers. They helped each other when one dropped a line, they assisted the other actors with costume changes and prop settings, and, at the end, grasped hands and took the most well-deserved bow I have ever seen on stage.

Involvement in extra-curricular activities does not have to be expensive, overly time consuming, or exhausting. It doesn't even have to be school related. Religious groups often offer activities for youths, generally requiring only a few hours per week worth of time. Get creative. If no school activities look interesting, try volunteering. Animal shelters, food banks, and hospitals are always in need of help with various duties.

The choice of extra-curricular activity matters little. What matters most is the student's enjoyment of it. Amazingly, the rest of the benefits simply fall into place!

6

Teens Need to Simplify Their Schedules

Sean Price

Sean Price has written many articles on education, history, politics, and labor.

Many teenagers enjoy the stress of a packed social and school calendar, but it is easy for students to go from busy to burnout. It is important for teens to find a healthy balance, and parents are instrumental in this.

Emily Rooney likes to keep busy. The 13-year-old from Quincy, Massachusetts, plays on three soccer teams. She also suits up for two hockey teams, runs cross-country, and plays basketball at school. At the same time, she participates in drama, chorus, and student council. Tuesday afternoons are devoted to church school. And Friday afternoons find Emily at a school club that helps kids in poor countries.

Sound hectic? "If you like doing all the stuff you do," Emily says, "it's never a problem."

Many teens agree. They prefer to pack in all the sports, clubs, and other extra activities they can. A recent University of Michigan study found that since 1981, there has been a sharp decrease in free time for kids. After homework, chores, and other duties, the amount of free time has shrunk by about 40 percent. Meanwhile, time spent in organized sports and other activities has risen dramatically. But experts warn that there is a limit to how much activity kids can handle.

Stress's Toll

"What happens when kids are overscheduled is that they get more stressed out, they get more irritable, they're lacking enough sleep, and in general their well-being is not as good," says William Doherty, a professor of family social science at the University of Minnesota.

Home life has suffered, too, in the last few decades, as family meals and vacations have fallen by the wayside. Now, many people are wondering whether young teens should be spending less time achieving and more time just living.

Many [parents] feel their kids need the extra edge that sports, music, and other activities provide.

One Activity After Another

Why are kids today busier than ever? Child-development expert Dorothy Sluss says that today's kids often have less freedom to run around and play by themselves. Parents fear crime even in well-off neighborhoods. Also, in many families, she says, both parents are likely to have jobs outside the home.

So kids take part in more after-school activities, like sports, games, and clubs. "Children are going to one activity after another in which they are competing," Sluss says. "There is a constant focus on competition."

Dr. Alvin Rosenfeld, a child psychiatrist, says that teens often shift themselves into overdrive. But parents get caught in the competitive cycle, too. Many feel their kids need the extra edge that sports, music, and other activities provide. Without it, a good college or the right job might be out of reach.

"Parenting has become the most competitive sport in America," Rosenfeld says.

From Busy to Burnout

William Doherty says that teens and parents have to find their own limits. "Some kids are very high energy and other kids need more time to kick back," he says. For both types, it can be hard to recognize when "busy" turns into "burnout."

The signs of burnout may include:

- Falling grades (although sometimes grades actually improve as teens struggle to keep up);

- Trouble staying awake in class, or relying too much on caffeine;

- Constant crabbiness at home or with friends.

Even the kids who seem to handle pressure best can burn out—or secretly desire to fail at something so that they will have time alone.

And ironically, a too-busy schedule may end up working against the ambitious student. Top colleges like to choose well-rounded, enthusiastic individuals, not necessarily students with a long list of activities. Overscheduled kids often find they don't have time to do their homework properly, and to really learn. A student with mediocre grades will not be a desirable candidate for many colleges.

It's OK to just do one or two things. This isn't a race.

Finding a Balance

Finding the proper balance can be tough. Scott Peterson, 13, of Chattanooga, Tennessee, takes a break when he feels overwhelmed. "Sometimes I feel like I'm getting cheated [out of free time] and kind of relax more when I'm supposed to be up doing other things," he says. Scott sometimes skips a martial-arts lesson or finds other wiggle room in his busy schedule.

Some researchers think the key is to encourage families to spend more time together and less time on the go.

Doherty, who helped found a group called Family Life First, says regular meals with no television should be a top goal. "This does not mean that if a family cannot have dinner together the kids are doomed," he says. "But they have to find other ways to connect."

At the same time, Dorothy Sluss insists, teens should look at ways to simplify their lives. "They don't have to be Superkid," she says. "It's OK if you just like science. It's OK if you just like books. It's OK to just do one or two things. This isn't a race."

7

Multitasking Hinders Teens' Analytical Abilities

Lori Aratani

Lori Aratani is a Washington Post *staff writer.*

While doing homework, many teens search the internet, call or text friends and do any number of things not to get bored. But even though this new generation is better at multitasking than previous ones, researchers fear that teenagers only learn to be good at being busy without deepening their knowledge. Studies suggest that today's teenagers lose their ability to focus and gain in-depth knowledge from their studies.

It's homework time and 17-year-old Megan Casady of Silver Spring [Maryland] is ready to study.

She heads down to the basement, turns on MTV and boots up her computer. Over the next half hour, Megan will send about a dozen instant messages discussing the potential for a midweek snow day. She'll take at least one cellphone call, fire off a couple of text messages, scan Weather.com, volunteer to help with a campus cleanup day at James Hubert Blake High School where she is a senior, post some comments on a friend's Facebook page and check out the new pom squad pictures another friend has posted on hers.

In between, she'll define "descent with modification" and explain how "the tree analogy represents the evolutionary relationship of creatures" on a worksheet for her AP [advanced placement] biology class.

Lori Arantani, "Teens Can Multitask, But What Are the Costs?" *washingtonpost.com*, February 26, 2007. Reprinted with permission of The Washington Post Writers Group.

Call it multitasking homework, Generation 'Net style.

Multitasking Prevents Focus

The students who do it say multitasking makes them feel more productive and less stressed. Researchers aren't sure what the long-term impact will be because no studies have probed its effect on teenage development. But some fear that the penchant for flitting from task to task could have serious consequences on young people's ability to focus and develop analytical skills.

There is special concern for teenagers because parts of their brain are still developing, said Jordan Grafman, chief of cognitive neuroscience at the National Institute of Neurological Disorders and Stroke.

"Introducing multitasking in younger kids in my opinion can be detrimental," he said. "One of the biggest problems about multitasking is that it's almost impossible to gain a depth of knowledge of any of the tasks you do while you're multitasking. And if it becomes normal to do, you'll likely be satisfied with very surface-level investigation and knowledge."

I'm able to accomplish more during an hour if I multitask.

Megan's parents, Steven and Donna Casady, might have their worries about the iPod/IM/text messaging/MTV effect on Megan's ability to retain the definition of "biochemical similarity," but they say it's hard to argue with a teenager who boasts a 3.85 unweighted grade-point average.

Organized Chaos

"To me, it's nothing but chaos," Steven Casady said. "But these kids? It seems to work for them. It seems to work for [Megan]. But it's hard for me to be in the same room when this is going on."

Thanks to the Internet, students say, facts are at their fingertips. If they get stuck on a math problem, they say, help is only an IM away.

"I honestly feel like I'm able to accomplish more during an hour if I multitask," said Christine Stoddard, 18, a senior at Yorktown High School in Arlington County [Virginia]. "If it's something like English or history that comes easily to me, then I can easily divide my attention. It's the way I've always been."

In fact, Christine sheepishly confessed that she was filling out a college scholarship application while being interviewed for this story.

Whatever the consequences of multitasking, they're going to be widespread. A recent report from the Kaiser Family Foundation found that when students are sitting in front of their computers "studying," they're also doing something else 65 percent of the time. In 1999, 16 percent of teenagers said they were "media multitaskers"—defined as using several type of media, such as television or computers, at once. By 2005, that percentage had increased to 26 percent. The foundation also found that girls were more likely to media multitask than boys.

The current generation of teens "is trying to do lots of multitasking because they think it's cool and less boring and because they have lots of gadgets that help them be more successful at this," said David Meyer, director of the Brain, Cognition and Action Laboratory at the University of Michigan. "The belief is they're getting good at this and that they're much better than the older generation at it and that there's no cost to their efficiency."

Research Inconclusive

Meyer, a psychologist and cognitive scientist who studies multitasking, has doubts.

"Kids who grow up under conditions where they have to multitask a lot may be developing styles of coping that would allow them to perform better in future environments where required to do a lot, but that doesn't mean their performance in the workplace would be better than if they were doing one thing at a time."

Researchers say there isn't any answer yet to whether multitasking helps, hurts or has no effect on teens' development.

"Given that kids have grown up always doing this, it may turn out that they are more skilled at it. We just don't know yet," said Russell Poldrack, an associate professor of psychology at the University of California at Los Angeles, who co-authored a study that examined multitasking and brain activity.

In Poldrack's study, volunteers in their 20s were given stacks of cards and asked to sort them. Then they were told to listen to a series of tones and identify the high-pitched ones while they sorted the cards. Researchers found that although there were similar success rates between the two groups when it came to sorting, when interviewed later, those who did not multitask were able to describe the cards in more detail.

Multitasking . . . could be especially detrimental for teenagers, who are still developing their ability to think and analyze information.

Poldrack said imaging showed that different parts of the brain were active depending on whether the subjects did single or multiple tasks. When subjects were focused on sorting, the hippocampus—the part of the brain responsible for storing and recalling information—was engaged. But when they were multitasking, that part of the brain was quiet and the part of the brain used to master repetitive skills—the striatum—was active.

Multitaskers "may not be building the same knowledge that they would be if they were focusing," Poldrack said. "While multitasking makes them feel like they are being more efficient, research suggests that there's very little you can do that involves multitasking that you can be as good at when you're not multitasking."

Meyer said if parts of the brain are less active when someone is multitasking, it could be especially detrimental for teenagers, who are still developing their ability to think and analyze information.

Superficial Knowledge

"They develop a more superficial style of study and may not learn material as well. What they get out of their study might be less deep," he said.

They might be getting goods grades, Meyer said, but there's a chance they could be getting better grades if they learned to focus on a single task or academic subject at a time.

Teens say they know there are limits.

Blake student Priscilla Tiglao, 17, is a multitasking blur when she sits down at her desk in the evening. But she says she will often forgo IM chats when it comes to AP chemistry or AP psychology—topics she finds more taxing. She might however, bend the rules for AP statistics.

Nane Tiglao, Priscilla's mother, is a nurse who is used to juggling multiple tasks. She talks on the phone while cooking and doing other chores. But when she watches her daughter—oy.

Still, she thinks, in the end this will be good for Priscilla.

"I think it's necessary for the future," Tiglao said. "This generation needs to multitask and to do it right. It's a good trait for anyone."

Meyer, a multitasker himself, agrees with some of that sentiment. Many jobs demand, even require, people to be multitaskers: air traffic controllers, bond traders, commodities brokers, to name a few.

"In that case, possibly the future's bright for these kids," he said. "But I think what's really needed in the future is a fairly heavy emphasis on learning and performing in different situations. If they want to be learning and performing under conditions of multitasking, then fine. But don't let them get away with just doing just that and completely losing out on other forms of learning."

8

Teens Must Learn How to Relax

Tracy Jan

Tracy Jan is an education reporter for The Boston Globe. *She writes about elementary and high school education in the Boston public schools as well as regional education trends.*

To relieve stress and help them cope, students at Fenway High School learn relaxation techniques. Gaining admittance to college, facing their parents' expectations, and dealing with the problems of violent inner city neighborhoods are all part of their daily experience. Many students are overwhelmed and require training to be able to focus on their studies. But some of the teenagers help pay their families' bills and find it hard to shut out the world in order to meditate.

As Andre Zayas lay on the hard gym floor, the 14-year-old from Dorchester struggled to clear his mind of his myriad burdens. He ached for a friend who was recently shot to death. He worried about finding a job to help his single mother pay the household bills. And in just a few hours, his project on the 1930s was due in humanities class, and he had not finished.

Next to him, Chanel Peguero closed her eyes and imagined graduating from high school in four years with a scholarship, the only way she would be able to afford college. The honor roll student cannot wait to escape her home in a South End housing development where her sleep is punctured by sirens, gunshots, and arguing adults.

Tracy Jan, "Stressed-Out Teens Get Lessons in Relaxing," *boston.com*, March 5, 2008. Reproduced by permission of The Boston Globe.

The teenagers, among two dozen Fenway High School freshmen arrayed in a semicircle beneath a basketball hoop, breathed deeply as a stress-reduction trainer instructed them on how to relax. New Age music floated through the gymnasium.

"Allow intruding thoughts to pass like clouds in the sky," said the trainer, Rana Chudnofsky, her soothing voice rising just above a whisper. "Take a minivacation from your day."

Helping Students Cope

Mind-body relaxation training, already popular among New England prep schools, is seeping into public high schools as principals and teachers worry about students' ever-mounting stress. In the most widescale effort in the state, specialists from Massachusetts General Hospital [MGH] have begun fanning out among urban and suburban high schools, including Boston, Needham, and Brookline, to help students cope.

"The kids are stressed out at every school, in every environment," said Marilyn Wilcher, senior director of the Benson-Henry Institute for Mind Body Medicine at MGH. "At Exeter, the stress is getting into Harvard. At the inner-city schools, it's whether they're going to be alive the next day."

In addition to deep breathing and visualizing their goals during gym class, the Fenway High students learned muscle-relaxation techniques and how to focus before a test by staring at the second hand of a clock for 30 to 60 seconds. In Needham, MGH is tracking a group of sophomores and juniors for a study measuring the impact of the training on students' anxiety and self-esteem.

All Students Suffer Stress

While high schools have always been pressure cookers, students say their stress is fueled by increased competition to gain admittance to selective colleges and demanding parental expectations. Others face more life-and-death anxieties as violence penetrates their neighborhoods.

Overtaxed and overcommitted students have more trouble understanding what they are supposed to be learning, said Paul Richards, principal of Needham High, who is at the forefront of the school stress-reduction movement. Students become so distracted and unable to focus that their academic performance plummets, he said.

"The culture drives this kind of anxiousness and this focus on the right grades and the right college," Richards said.

The principal of the high-achieving affluent suburban school 20 minutes west of Boston drew national attention [in 2007] after he ended the publication of the honor roll in the local newspaper, to reduce pressure on students.

Parents Hinder Relaxation

On top of peer pressure, some students believe that parents contribute to stress. They complain of "helicopter parents" who obsessively monitor their children's attendance and grades via a website set up by the school. Students said their teachers routinely field calls from parents inquiring about tests and assignments before the students have a chance to log on and check their grades.

Relaxation training boosted grade point averages and test scores and improved student time-management skills and attendance.

"Definitely our generation of parents are following our kids more closely than our parents did," said Wendy Perlman, whose son is a Needham High junior. "But most parents are very well meaning and aware of overstepping their place. It's a very small minority that are actually driving the kids crazy."

Perlman urged her son to sign up for the monthlong stress-reduction workshop as part of the multiyear Benson-Henry/MGH research. The institute is paying $35,000 for the

Needham study through grants. Other schools, which are not part of the study, pay $2,500 to $25,000 for workshops.

Relaxation Boosts Grades

Some parents and educators fear that the focus on stress might erode students' drive to achieve.

But a Benson-Henry study in the late 1990s of students in South Central Los Angeles middle schools showed that relaxation training boosted grade point averages and test scores and improved student time-management skills and attendance. . . .

[In Needham,] it is unclear whether the exercises are sticking.

For Danny Blackman, stress comes in bursts. The 16-year-old Needham junior is enrolled in accelerated and Advanced Placement classes and hopes to attend Cornell University, his father's alma mater. His weeknights and weekends are consumed by school clubs: speech and debate, mock trial, and Model Congress. Then there are his SAT prep classes and driving school.

Blackman says his stress festers when multiple academic deadlines clash with his extracurricular activities, as happened one night when he had to study for an AP history test on the Roaring '20s and write an English paper on *The Great Gatsby*. But instead of tapping into the relaxation techniques he has learned, Blackman powered through the night without a break.

"The thing about relaxation is it takes 10 to 20 minutes to put on some weird CD or do a breathing exercise," he said. "I honestly don't want to take the time to do that when I have to finish an English paper."

But classmate Jenny Huezo-Rosales, 16, said she regularly uses the relaxation techniques to help her decompress. She has trouble focusing on school work at home because she shares a room with six siblings. Now, her siblings know to leave her in peace when she turns out the lights, lies on her bed, and shuts her eyes for 10 minutes.

Schedules Too Crowded

At Fenway High, a small Boston public school where most students are college-bound, gym teacher Julio Avila invited the stress trainer to work with his freshmen because he sees students struggling with a host of nonacademic stresses.

"They have jobs after school," Avila said. "They have to baby-sit their siblings. They're concerned about safety in their neighborhoods. And they don't have the luxury of having parents who drive them to swimming and gymnastics programs after school."

Zayas, the Dorchester teenager who worries about helping his mother pay the bills, said his stress is manifesting in a regular nightmare that his mother, on her deathbed, asks him to look after his younger brother and cousin. He says he wakes up crying in the middle of the night.

"When you have no father in the household, you have to realize that you're pretty much the alpha male," he said. "You have a responsibility. You have people that you have to look after."

During the workshop, Zayas filled out a worksheet of stress warning signals, checking off nearly all the symptoms. He bites his nails, sleeps a lot, and has frequent headaches. He lashes out by yelling or swearing, avoids friends, and has a hard time making decisions.

He was grateful for the opportunity to escape from his troubles. But relief was temporary.

"I'm still stressed," he said before leaving for his next class. "All the weight is on my shoulders."

9

After-School Programs Can Help Teens Succeed Academically

Joe Beck

Joe Beck is a staff writer for Gazette.Net, *the online site of Maryland community newspapers.*

Many students' grades seem to suffer because of a lack of involvement. They see the school as a bureaucratic institution with little to offer on an individual level. At Seneca Valley High School in Germantown, Maryland, the Sports Academy is trying to change that. The program offers sports, trips to parks and plays, and adult supervision and help with homework. The experiment has so far been a success, and participants report higher grade point averages than in previous years.

A recently introduced after-school program at Seneca Valley High School is winning praise from students and school officials for improving grades and attitudes toward academics.

"It's all positive," said Alan Fathi, a sophomore who believes the Sports Academy program contributed to a dramatic rise in his grades since it began in February [2008]. "I have nothing bad to say. I would recommend it to all schools."

Fathi is one of 75 to 150 students who show up in the school cafeteria from 2:30 to 5 *p.m.* four days a week to participate in the Sports Academy, a county-run recreation

Joe Beck, "Sports Academy Helps Struggling Teens," *Gazette.Net*, May 14, 2008. Reproduced by permission.

program focused on improving their academic performance and keeping them out of trouble.

"We love the program," said Principal Suzanne Maxey. "A lot of kids are involved in it. It's very well supervised and well organized."

Changing Student Attitudes

Despite its name, the Sports Academy encompasses far more than sports. The program mixes adult supervision and academic help with a wide variety of leisure opportunities ranging from video games, flag football and basketball to weekend trips to amusement parks and plays.

The program is open to all students, but much of it is designed to encourage students struggling with grades or showing signs of getting into trouble with the law to change their attitudes and behavior. Students need parental permission to participate.

A Montgomery County police officer was among the nine adults in the cafeteria supervising the students on Monday; the others came from the recreation department. An on-duty officer is assigned to work with students each day the program runs.

"The Sports Academy started out to address the gang issue," said Melanie Coffin, manager of the recreation department's teen team. "Many of our students we know are gang involved. That's why the police play such a large role with us."

Students . . . offered . . . praise for the way the program has helped them look at school in a way that encourages them to work harder while enjoying new activities.

John Quarless, a recreation specialist with the department who leads the Sports Academy at Seneca Valley, said he believes much of the program's success can be attributed to the trustful relationships the supervising adults have with the students.

"We listen more than we preach," Quarless said.

Getting Help with Academics

In an interview in the cafeteria at the conclusion of the day's program, Fathi said the program's combination of sports and fun has worked for him, noting that he entered the program in February with a grade point average of 1.0 that he has since raised to 3.0. He attributed the difference to help he receives with his homework.

"Everything is going uphill for me now," he said. "Everything is positive."

His fellow students, Mohammad Sayyad, Justin Randolph and Tawina Zulu, all offered similar praise for the way the program has helped them look at school in a way that encourages them to work harder while enjoying new activities.

Sayyad, a freshman, said his GPA has gone from 1.71 to 2.8. Randolph, a sophomore, said he has raised his from 1.85 to 2.71 and Zulu, also a sophomore, said she improved from 1.76 to 2.0. Equally important, she said, was the opportunity to participate in group leadership activities that she believes will strengthen her college applications.

"I've been a lot more focused on my grades. They really push me a lot, and it makes a difference," Zulu said.

The Sports Academy is part of a larger effort to bring more after-school recreation to upcounty [Montgomery County, Maryland,] after years of focus on the downcounty, Coffin said. The program at Seneca Valley is the sixth in the county—the first upcounty.

Another county after-school program, RecExtra, has begun reaching upcounty schools in the last two years [2006–2008], including Roberto Clemente Middle School in Germantown.

RecExtra differs from the Sports Academy by funding after-school programs that are organized and staffed by teachers and school support staff.

Engaged Students Perform Better

Coffin said problems linked to lack of English-speaking skills, low income and gang activity led county officials to focus the first Sports Academy programs on downcounty schools.

[In 2007], they began studying schools upcounty as sites for further expansion. They considered information from police and the county executive's office, student grade point averages and the ability and willingness of schools to form a partnership with the recreation department, Coffin said. All of the factors led them to Seneca Valley, she said.

Shawn Joseph, the principal at Clemente, estimated that RecExtra helps pay for programs involving 150 to 200 students. He cited clubs for Spanish, chess, Latin cooking, male and female mentoring and homework as some of RecExtra's main beneficiaries.

Joseph attributed a 61 percent drop in suspensions at Clemente [in 2008] partly to the advantages of RecExtra.

"When you have kids more engaged and more connected to school, they tend to socially behave better, which in turn brings better academic results," Joseph said.

Coffin said close study of the Sports Academy program at downcounty schools showed that its participants were making academic gains. Some raised their grade point averages and others "went from zero percent homework turned in to 100 percent," she said.

10

Sports Should Not Be the Main Focus in High School

Mary Tedrow

Mary Tedrow is the codirector of the Northern Virginia Writing Project. She teaches English and journalism at Millbrook High School in Winchester, Virginia.

Most high school athletes never make it into professional sports, yet year after year high schools around the country spend a disproportionate amount of money on varsity sports while neglecting academics. Only twenty percent of the student population are athletes, and yet they demand the financial backing and moral support that more academically inclined students lack. Sports are important, but schools should shift their focus to help their students succeed in their professional careers and stimulate their intellectual development.

When our high school student newspaper earned top honors in the state, it excited the athletic director. As the Keeper of All Things Competitive, he also checked our ranking in a state awards program for schools with top academic honors. He found that we had beaten the neighboring schools and were ranked fifth in the state.

"Maybe," he told me, without a trace of irony, "we could become known as an academic school!"

Maybe, indeed, but not likely.

I consider myself an athlete—a runner for 30 years, tennis player, and competitive gymnast during high school. But it

Mary Tedrow, "High School Sports: Who's the Real Loser?" *Teacher Magazine*, March 20, 2007. Reproduced by permission of Editorial Projects in Education.

dismays me that, when it comes to decision-making at the school level, on every field of play, sports wins and academics loses. For all of our hand-wringing over NCLB [No Child Left Behind] reports, a school with a winning football or basketball team trumps negative headlines about test scores every time.

Sports Beat Out Academics

Though America loves its sports, the inclusion of extracurricular sports is in direct conflict with the academic pursuits of a high school. The proof? Here are a few instances where I've seen sports take the field and routinely triumph over sound instructional choices:

- In a discussion about aligning our start time with the later elementary school start to match the late-riser rhythm of adolescents: "We can't. It would push the sports' practice times back too late."

- In considering year-round school, with its proven benefits in overcoming learning losses during long summer breaks: "It will interfere with the sports seasons."

- In a choice between two teachers for an academic leadership role (and extra pay)—one highly qualified versus one with so-so credentials but a winning record as football coach—football wins.

- During the all-important reviews for state testing, kids are routinely excused when state sporting competition is on the line.

- While we give lip service to reducing classroom interruptions, instructional time is regularly disrupted by pep rallies, early travel to sporting events, and overnight sports travel.

- To survive intense sporting seasons, some coaches who teach cut back on assignments, shuffle grading off to student assistants, and excuse themselves from professional development opportunities.

Sports Nearly Always Favored

These are the conflicts for schools that maintain high-cost, high-profile extracurricular sports programs. The pendulum nearly always swings to favor sports, even though they only impact about 20 percent of the student body. (At the next pep rally, note how many students sit glumly in the stands to cheer on the same 40–50 students they've celebrated season after season. This year at my school the score is pep rallies: 3; assemblies for music, art or drama: 0.)

The argument for sports goes like this: *It's the only thing keeping some kids in school.* Though I've yet to see any statistic supporting this contention, I *have* seen capable students coast through classes as they place their emphasis on an athletic career. Some hang their future prospects on a sport, letting marketable skills like effective reading and writing stagnate.

When education funds are no longer diverted to transportation, uniforms, and maintaining interest in sports, both the energy and resources could be used to improve instruction.

At my school, most of the competitive athletes are also competitive students, a lucky elite who benefit from the rich genetic soup that is their makeup. A major sporting event held during the school day can cut attendance in an Advanced Placement class in half.

An Unrealistic Message

But it is the at-risk student whom the sports argument supposedly defends, and these students often bank on sports to carry them past other disadvantages like poverty or poor study habits. Because the system sometimes bends over backwards to keep high-performing athletes in school, the unrealistic message sent to impressionable youth is that athleticism can carry them through life. But even with outstanding athletic skills, a single injury can quickly end any hope of a career. In my 17-year career, reaching roughly 1,500 students, the number who have gone on to careers as professional athletes is exactly zero.

One at-risk student dutifully sat in my 9th grade English class for four years—but only through the fall football season. His high school career ended after he reached the limits of his eligibility, and he began his next career in prison.

I like sports. I also think that the best coaches generally make excellent teachers. I know I am at my best when my teaching resembles coaching rather than lecturing. But the emphasis on the athletic program does affect instruction.

What would happen if resources for sports were removed from schools and consolidated into single sporting complexes where we supported community teams? When education funds are no longer diverted to transportation, uniforms, and maintaining interest in sports, both the energy and resources could be used to improve instruction. Those who wanted to teach and coach could do so, taking on coaching as the second job it truly is. The community would have a clear picture of the true cost of sporting programs when the funding is separated.

As a result, kids might actually want to come to school, not to play ball, but because the increased attention to instruction will help every student succeed and find a skill to translate into a lifetime of learning and earning. And for many, I'm sure, a lifetime of enjoying and participating in sporting events.

11

Volunteering Gives Students an Edge on College Applications

Reecy Aresty

Reecy Aresty is a financial advisor and college admissions/ financial aid expert.

Starting in ninth grade, students should be joining student clubs to become well-rounded college applicants. It is important to find a good fit early, since changing clubs might influence a college admissions officer negatively. Taking leadership rolls in a Debate Club or the Key Club will allow students to gain valuable experiences. Volunteering, too, is an integral part of creating a successful résumé and can give college applicants an edge over competitors with a similar grade point average.

[In] 9th grade the student should begin clubbing. No, I don't mean staying out 'til the wee hours of the morning partying. Membership in the Debate Club, Student Council, Key Club, etc., is one of the absolute necessities to becoming a well-rounded, acceptable student.

During their entire high school career, it will prove to be even more beneficial if the student holds office or takes on a leadership role in some of these clubs. Better still, at some point students should take the initiative and form their own volunteer organization(s), or perhaps a fundraiser for a disadvantaged family or someone who was struck down with a dis-

Reecy Aresty, "Extracurricular Activities," *Getting into College and Paying for It,* June 29, 2003. Reproduced by permission.

ease that requires a substantial dollar amount for treatment. Clubbing, participating in sports, and getting involved in everyday school activities all add points to the GPA.

Clubbing is fun and builds character at the same time. However, rather than joining a different club every semester, it is far more impressive to stay with the same club for all four years. This will show admissions officers that the student has perseverance and honors commitments. It's very important to show your passion about something other than just the opposite sex. Admissions officers are looking to test the student's resolve and their ability to finish what they start—whatever they start.

Beginning early is also very important, because if a club doesn't have the right fit, you need to know by the end of the 9th grade or at the very latest, the 10th grade, rather than in the senior year. By the end of the 10th grade, the student should have narrowed down their club involvement allowing them more time to take an active role in the ones they've chosen.

Making Connections

I always recommend joining the Yearbook Staff, Debate Club and the Key Club. By being a member, or even better, being an officer, students get to be more involved with the entire school and can develop relationships with teachers that will prove invaluable when it comes time for LOR's (letters of recommendation). Being president of a language club also goes a long way with an admissions committee.

Leadership is a quality that will impress others throughout a student's life. Taking on a leadership role demonstrates taking a risk and assuming responsibility. Even students who are super athletes need some diversity, as sports alone are not enough; students need to avoid the impression that they are one-dimensional. It is more important that students are portrayed as multi-faceted.

Volunteering and Community Service

The student must also begin to accumulate community service or volunteer hours, which will add even more points to their overall GPA. However, don't confuse extracurricular activities with volunteer work. One has nothing to do with the other. I define extracurricular activities as in-school participation. Community service takes place outside of school.

Such activities involve scouting, working for one's house of worship, working with AIDS and/or Alzheimer's patients, seniors, hospice, Special Olympics, the blind, assisting hospital or nursing home staffs, coaching, refereeing, tutoring, Horses For The Handicapped (autistic children), or any other involvement with the handicapped, Habitat for Humanity, Meals On Wheels, environmental work, such as cleaning up beaches and highways, etc., etc., etc.

Showing Compassion

By participating in volunteer work with financially, emotionally and/or intellectually challenged people, students demonstrate their compassion and empathy for others, and this will help them shine with the admissions officers. Working with those who are less fortunate also gives the student a much broader idea of what life outside of their own environment is actually like.

Legendary comic George Burns used to say, "Every day I go into the kitchen, sit down at the table, open the newspaper to the obituaries, and, if my name isn't there—I eat breakfast!" Well, I'm certainly no comic, but each morning I go into my kitchen, sit down at the table, and read three local newspapers. I cut out and save all of the numerous volunteer opportunities listed. As a result, I have compiled literally thousands of volunteer listings, and I encourage parents and their students to come in and browse through the file to find unlimited possibilities for volunteer work. I strongly recommend that every student scour his or her own local newspaper(s) for such listings.

Many religious and other organizations have been known to give double credit for volunteer hours. Try it yourself. The colleges will love you for participating above and beyond the call of duty.

The more community service hours, the more of a decisive advantage a student has in the admissions process.

Graduation from a public high school in Florida usually requires a minimum of 40 hours of community service, and school districts throughout the country each have their own specific requirements.

Additionally, many private and religious schools have no mandatory requirements. Don't make the mistake of ignoring or only completing the minimum. An example of the benefits of community service is best demonstrated in this scenario:

Two students apply to the same college, but there's only room for one of them. They have comparable grades and test scores. Student "A" has 370 hours of community service, while student "B" has only 40 hours. Which student do you think will most likely be accepted?

Volunteering Pays Off

This rhetorical question illustrates a very important point. The more community service hours, the more of a decisive advantage a student has in the admissions process. As part of a student's resume, it is a safe bet that many schools will actually look for student involvement with the handicapped or others less fortunate.

Students who start their own fundraiser or other similar community service project will virtually guarantee extra points being added to their GPA. This is so well regarded by the schools; it can actually make up for a shortfall on the transcript! It is here that mediocrity fails and a degree of excellence overwhelms.

Warning! If you're on a sports team, in the orchestra, or have a parent who is a physician, don't limit your time to only those particular activities. Once again, it is here that diversity as well as commitment counts.

A combination of work, community service and sports cover all the bases. Don't ask yourself, "How can I possibly do all of that?" I guarantee that there are numerous other students doing more. How isn't important, but why is! That's what the best schools are looking for—above average students who go the extra distance. What all students should be asking themselves is, "Will I be one of them?"—and do what it takes, whatever it takes, to make sure that they are.

No one plans to fail, but sadly, too many fail to plan.

In 2003, two students whom I counseled had each accumulated over 1,000 hours of community service. One was a Sea Scout and an Eagle Scout, and the other had achieved the same status in the Girl Scouts and also had accrued hundreds of additional volunteer hours.

Another student of mine who is legally blind, bilingual, had over 1,200 service hours, 1,400+ SAT, 4.5+ GPA, etc., etc., etc.! This is a perfect example of what a student with the proper guidance and motivation can accomplish.

Success Results from Planning

Planning is the key word that not only sums up the admissions process but the entire college financial aid process as well. You plan your work and work your plan. No one plans to fail, but sadly, too many fail to plan.

Parents and their ninth graders reading this book will now have a tremendous advantage over families with seniors who haven't done much planning, even if their students have impressive numbers. Starting early also narrows down college choices so that by the 12th grade, students will know exactly which schools they'll be applying to. It's here that curriculum counts and name recognition is secondary. The one overriding factor that families need to be aware of is to insure that the student obtains the maximum knowledge in the course they are pursuing!

How you spend the next three summers will also have a direct effect on how the admissions officers will perceive you. A lackluster summer suggests the student is not community oriented, and this could actually detract from the GPA. Students volunteering for out-of-state community service (excluding summer camp) will certainly turn heads.

If you are fortunate enough to be able to tour Europe or the Far East, keep a diary of your everyday activities. Accentuate the cultural aspects of your trip, rather than the leisure times. If you studied in a foreign country, that would be an A+. Don't squander such opportunities. These experiences will be great material for future college essays.

Taking college courses in the summer is another great idea. This also shows risk taking, which, once again, is highly regarded by all admissions officers. If the student can land an internship, that too would be most advantageous and will add to the GPA. Just be sure that the work suits the student's academic abilities. Students should not be afraid to quit if all they are doing is inventory or some other menial task.

12

High Achievers Might Be Paying a Steep Price

Carleton Kendrick

Carleton Kendrick is a family therapist and consultant.

Many college applicants come to their campus interview well-coached and painstakingly prepared. But many don't seem to know why they are undergoing rigorous testing or why they played sports or kept volunteering throughout high school. Lost in creating a good résumé and excelling at exams are personality and fun. Instead of trying to become picture-perfect mini-adults, teenagers should have the opportunity to explore their own interests. They should strive less and be more curious about their own expectations and goals.

They come to me with SATs pushing 1600 and more awards than military heroes. The valedictorians. The student leaders. The super-jocks. They are applying to Harvard. They are the children you want your kids to become.

For the past 17 years, I've been an alumni interviewer for Harvard. As part of its admissions process, Harvard extends applicants an opportunity to meet with one of its alumni. To personalize the process. To allow its applicants to "come alive," apart from their strategically packaged portfolios.

Acknowledging that most teens walk into these interviews with understandably heightened anxiety, my initial focus is on helping them exhale their fears and worries about impressing

Carleton Kendrick, "High Achievers: What Price Are They Paying?" *Family Education*, July 10, 2008. Reproduced by permission of Family Education Network.

me. "We're here so that Harvard can get to know you a little better. There are no right or wrong answers. We're just going to chat for a while," I offer calmly.

I try to get beyond their Miss America-like, rehearsed responses—"Harvard is the best environment available for me to pursue my pre-medical studies." I'm looking for clues as to whether they'd make considerate roommates, inquisitive scholars, and generous contributors to Harvard's community. Most often, these frightened, pressured high-achievers have trouble finding their own voice. Instead, I hear them speak in the boilerplate, programmed, success-oriented words of their parents, teachers and college coaches.

Running on Empty

He listed cross-country as a sport he took up in his junior year. No athletic endeavors had preceded his high-school running. I asked John (all names have been changed) what had drawn him to distance running and why he came to pursue it his junior year. He replied matter-of-factly, "My guidance counselor told me it would look good on my transcript if I had a sport. He said that colleges looked for well-rounded kids and that I needed something like a sport to look better for colleges. Time was running out and my junior year was the last year I could get a sport in before I sent in my applications. I joined cross-country because everyone makes it who tries out." "Do you like running? Does it give you pleasure?" I hoped. "No," was his hollow reply.

Peter had scored two 800s on his SATs and was recognized as a National Merit Scholar. As we spoke of his favorite high-school classes, I asked whether he had ever challenged any of his English teachers' opinions in class. Looking down at the floor, he spoke softly. "Sure, I used to disagree lots of times. I mean, there's no absolute right answer when it comes to knowing whether an author was using her own life or not as the basis for the main character, right? But every time I'd disagree with this teacher or our textbook's opinion I'd end up getting marked down for it. So I learned it's better to tell teachers what they want to hear so you'll get a better grade." Sadly, there was no anger or disappointment in his voice.

Programmed to Succeed

Sarah, class valedictorian and winner of numerous, prestigious math and science awards, spoke with a dull and disembodied affect about her academic triumphs and her future, "Math and science have always been easy for me. I don't like them nearly as much as literature but they're what I do best. I guess I'll major in them in college, get a graduate degree in them and then get an engineering job and get married. That's what my parents (survivors of Cambodia's killing fields) expect. They want me to get an engineering job and to get married as soon as I get my graduate degree. I hope that I can save up enough money so that I can retire early, like in my 50s, and travel." Sarah was 17, a broken sparrow, dying to be middle-aged.

How do you raise kids to be high achievers without their suffering anxiety, dread, and abject resignation? Stop hurrying and stealing their childhood, structuring and scheduling their every waking moment.

Stressed for Success

Heard enough? I have. Over the past two decades, the children I've interviewed have become progressively more packaged for success. They've been advised, scared, and professionally coached into believing that school's only purpose is to get the grades that will gain them admission into an elite college. College must then result in a degree that translates into a high-paying job and a secure financial future. That's the plan. The only plan. It's no wonder that a recently released American

Council on Education survey of more than 348,000 college freshmen reports that, "Academic credentials, rather than a love of learning, seem to be their motivation." Shame on us all.

We begin telling kids by eighth, or ninth grade, "It all counts now! Every grade, every sports performance, every activity in or out of school. You're building your permanent record for college. It's time to get serious." As one student explained, "The big transcript worries start freshman year and your whole future is pretty much determined by the end of junior year in high school." We actually start scaring them much earlier than middle school. I've got a list of third-and fourth-grade therapy clients who have seen me for school-related stress to prove it.

Free to Be

So how do you raise kids to be high achievers without their suffering anxiety, dread, and abject resignation? Stop hurrying and stealing their childhood, structuring and scheduling their every waking moment; read or re-read David Elkind's prophetic, cautionary, *The Hurried Child: Growing Up Too Fast Too Soon.* Don't frighten them into believing in and following your master plan for academic and career success. Begin telling them as preschoolers that you love and admire them for who they are, not for the grades and achievements that they bring you. Encourage their own natural academic and extra-curricular interests, regardless of whether they are deemed portfolio-advisable by costly college "handlers." Urge them to volunteer and to serve others and do so together—as part of your family's values, not because it will look good on their college transcripts. In short, love and support them as they challenge and search for themselves, fulfill their dreams and become the people they choose to be.

Organizations to Contact

The editors have compiled the following list of organizations concerned with the issues debated in this book. The descriptions are derived from materials provided by the organizations. All have publications or information available for interested readers. The list was compiled on the date of publication of the present volume; the information provided here may change. Be aware that many organizations take several weeks or longer to respond to inquiries, so allow as much time as possible.

America's Promise Alliance
1110 Vermont Ave. NW, Washington, DC   20005
(202) 657-0600 • fax: (202) 657-0601
Web site: www.americaspromise.org

The America's Promise Alliance works to uphold the "five promises" it makes to children: caring adults, safe places, a healthy start, an effective education and opportunities to help others—at home, in school and in the community. It publishes newsletters and reports online.

ASNE High School Journalism Initiative
11690B Sunrise Valley Drive., Reston, VA   20191-1409
fax: (703) 453-1139
Web site: www.highschooljournalism.org

The ASNE High School Journalism Initiative helps scholastic journalism to grow a diverse generation of new journalists. ASNE is a membership organization of top U.S. newspaper editors. It publishes news written by teens on its Web site.

ED—U.S. Department of Education

400 Maryland Ave. SW, Washington, DC   20202
(800) USA-LEARN
Web site: www.ed.gov/students/landing.jhtml

ED—a special branch of the U.S. Department of Education—was created to promote student achievement and preparation for global competitiveness by working to foster educational excellence and ensure equal access. It collects data on America's schools and distributes research, while taking measures against discrimination and for equal access to education. Newsletters are available online, and reports and brochures on education can be ordered on ED's Web site.

Helping America's Youth (HAY)

The White House, Washington, DC   20500
(202) 456-1414 • fax: (202) 456-2461
Web site: www.helpingamericasyouth.gov

Helping America's Youth is a nationwide effort to raise awareness about the challenges facing our youth, particularly at-risk boys, and to motivate caring adults to connect with youth in three key areas: family, school, and community. HAY was founded by First Lady Laura Bush and has resulted in collaboration across ten federal agencies, including the Departments of Agriculture, Commerce, Education, Health and Human Services, Housing and Urban Development, Interior, Justice, and Labor; the Corporation for National and Community Service; and the Office of National Drug Control Policy. HAY provides resources and information on their initiatives online.

National Center for Education Statistics (NCES)

1990 K St. NW, Washington, DC   20006
(202) 502-7300
Web site: www.nces.ed.gov

The NCES, located within the U.S. Department of Education and the Institute of Education Sciences, is the primary federal entity for collecting and analyzing data related to education. Newsletters and research reports are available online.

U.S. Department of Labor

Frances Perkins Bldg., Washington, DC   20210

(866) 4-USA-DOL

Web site: www.dol.gov

The U.S. Department of Labor publishes news, laws, union reports, and event calendars on its Web site. It also maintains a site for youth-related issues at www.youthrules.dol.gov.

U.S. Department of State, Bureau of Educational and Cultural Affairs, Youth Programs Division

e-mail: ecawebsitesmail@state.gov

Web site: http://exchanges.state.gov/education/citizens/students

The Youth Programs Division works to establish long-lasting ties between the United States and other countries through exchange programs and institutional partnerships. Programs focus primarily on secondary schools and promote mutual understanding, leadership development, educational transformation, and democratic ideals. News about its programs appear regularly online.

Youth Service America (YSA)

1101 Fifteenth St. NW, Suite 200, Washington, DC   20005

Web site: www.ysa.org

Youth Service America is a resource center that partners with thousands of organizations committed to increasing the quality and quantity of volunteer opportunities for young people aged five to twenty-five to serve locally, nationally, and globally. A newsletter and the *YSA Quarterly* are available online.

Youth Volunteer Network

Web site: www.networkforgood.youthnoise.com

Network for Good is a nonprofit organization dedicated to using the Web to help people get more involved in their communities—from volunteering and donating money, to speaking out on important issues. YouthNOISE is an online community of young people where they discuss issues and plan to take action. Stories and comments by teens are regularly published online.

Bibliography

Books

A. Bell and D. Smith — *Developing Leadership Abilities: Personal and Professional Development.* Upper Saddle River, NJ: Prentice-Hall, 2002.

W.G. (Buzz) Bissinger — *Saturday Night Lights: A Town, a Team, and a Dream.* Cambridge, MA: Da Capo Press, 2004.

P. Bronson — *What Should I Do with My Life? The True Story of People Who Answered the Ultimate Question.* New York: Random House, 2002.

Bradford Brown — *The World's Youth: Adolescence in Eight Regions of the Globe.* Cambridge: Cambridge University Press, 2002.

Carol Carter, Joyce Bishop, and Sara Lyman — *Keys to Success in College, Career, and Life: How to Achieve Your Goals.* Upper Saddle River, NJ: Prentice-Hall, 2003.

R. Cohen-Sandler — *Stressed-Out Girls: Helping Them Thrive in the Age of Pressure.* New York: Viking, 2005.

Mihaly Csikszentmihalyi and Barbara Schneider — *Becoming Adult: How Teenagers Prepare for the World of Work.* New York: Basic Books, 2003.

Skip Downing	*On Course: Strategies for Creating Success in College and Life.* Boston: Houghton Mifflin, 2002.
Dave Ellis	*Becoming a Master Student.* Boston: Houghton Mifflin, 2002.
Mikki Halpin	*It's Your World—If You Don't Like It, Change It: Activism for Teenagers.* New York: Simon Pulse, 2004.
JIST	*Creating Your High School Portfolio: An Interactive School, Career, and Life Planning.* Indianapolis: JIST, 2003.
Jean Johnson and Ann Duffett	*Life After High School: Young People Talk About Their Hopes and Prospects.* New York: Public Agenda, 2005.
Murray Milner	*Freaks, Geeks, and Cool Kids: American Teenagers, Schools, and the Culture of Consumption.* New York: Routledge, 2004.
Jeylan Mortimer	*Working and Growing Up in America.* Cambridge, MA: Harvard University Press, 2005.
A. Raptis	*The Empowered Student.* Malibu, CA: Successmakers, 2000.
Alexandra Robbins	*The Overachievers: The Secret Lives of Driven Kids.* New York: Hyperion, 2007.
Alvin Rosenfeld and Nicole Wise	*The Over-Scheduled Child: Avoiding the Hyper-Parenting Trap.* New York: St. Martin's, 2001.

Michael Sadowski   *Adolescents at School: Perspectives on Youth, Identity, and Education.* Cambridge: Harvard Education Press, 2003.

Traci Truly   *Teen Rights: A Legal Guide for Teens and the Adults in Their Lives.* Naperville, IL: Sphinx, 2002.

Periodicals

Armelle Vincent Arriola   "Teen Busting," *Reclaiming Children and Youth,* 2001.

Tony Baranek   "Hunger on Hold," *U.S. Society and Values: Sports in America,* December 2003.

B. Barber, J. Eccles, J. and M. Stone   "Whatever Happened to the Jock, the Brain, and the Princess? Young Adult Pathways Linked to Adolescent Activity Involvement and Social Identity," *Journal of Adolescent Research,* vol. 16, 2001.

Tom Carson   "The Kids Are All Right: Teens Aren't as Warped as Some of the Books About Them," *Atlantic Monthly,* July 2004.

Centers for Disease Control and Prevention   "Participation in High School Physical Education—United States, 1991–2003," *Morbidity and Mortality Weekly Report,* September 16, 2004.

Janine Certo, Kathleen Cauley, and Carl Chafin   "Students' Perspectives on Their High School Experience," *Adolescence,* vol. 38, 2003.

Esther Chang
et al.

"What Do They Want in Life? The Life Goals of a Multi-Ethnic, Multi-Generational Sample of High School Seniors," *Journal of Youth and Adolescence*, June 2006.

N. De Biasi

"Why Are Teens Stressed?" California State Science Fair Project Abstract, 2003.

Jeanne Elium
and Don Elium

"Raising a Teenager: Parents and the Nurturing of a Responsible Teen," *Adolescence*, Winter 2007.

Kenneth Gray

"Is High School Career and Technical Education Obsolete?" *Phi Delta Kappan*, November 2004.

Mia Hamm

"My Own Words: On Self-Esteem and Sports," *eJournalUSA: Global Issues—Growing Up Healthy*, January 2005.

Richard Hannah
and Charles
Baum

"An Examination of College-Bound High School Students' Labor Market Behavior: Why Some Students Work and Why Some Do Not," *Education*, vol. 121, no. 4, 2001.

Froma Harrop

"Jobs for Teens: A Stimulating Idea," *Seattle Times*, June 2, 2008.

Marianne Hurst

"Leading the Way: Student-Run Foundations Across the Country Are Empowering a New Generation of Teenagers to Play Larger Roles in Their Schools and Communities," *Education Week*, April 20, 2005.

Marvin Lewis   "My Own Words: On Finding Your
                      Way," *eJournalUSA: Global
                      Issues—Growing Up Healthy*, January
                      2005.

Isabel Lyman   "Teen Success Begins at Home:
                      Adolescence Is a Troubled Time, but
                      Home Education Offers Benefits for
                      Young People When They Need It
                      Most—as Illustrated by the Success
                      Stories of Four Homeschooled
                      Teens," *New American*, June 17, 2002.

S. Rollin et al.   "A Stress Management Curriculum
                      for At-Risk Youth," *Journal of
                      Humanistic Counseling, Education
                      and Development*, vol. 42, 2003.

H. Taras   "Physical Activity and Student
                      Performance at School," *Journal of
                      School Health*, vol. 75, no. 6, 2005.

Katherine Torres   "Teens at Work: Challenges in
                      Protecting a Young Work Force,"
                      Occupational Hazards, May 2006.

Rona Wilensky   "College Is Not for Everyone,"
                      Education Week, April 20, 2005.

Elke Zeijl et al.   "The Role of Parents and Peers in
                      the Leisure Activities of Young
                      Adolescents," *Journal of Leisure
                      Research*, vol. 32, no. 3, 2000.

Index